21 DIWALI RECIPES

Quick & Easy,
Snacks & Sweets.

REKHA SINGH

Copyright © 2017 REKHA SINGH

All rights reserved.

ISBN: **9781549979620**
ISBN-13:

DEDICATION

This is my first cookbook and I would like to dedicate it to my husband for believing, encouraging, understanding and tolerating me through the whole process. He is the bedrock of my life.

CONTENTS

	Acknowledgments	i
1	BESAN LADDU	Pg 1
2	NACHNI AND OATS LADDU	Pg 3
3	SOOJI or RAVA LADDU	Pg 5
4	WHEAT or CHURMA LADDU	Pg 6
5	COCONUT BURFI	Pg 8
6	KALAKAND BURFI	Pg 9
7	MAWA GUJIYA/ KARANJI	Pg 10
8	MAWA GUJIYA STUFFING	Pg 12
9	SHANKARPALI	Pg 14
10	BUTTER CHAKLI	Pg 15
11	MASALA CHAKLI	Pg 17

12	WHEAT CHAKLI	Pg 19
13	GATHIYA	Pg 21
14	POHA CHIVDA	Pg 23
15	ALMOND DROP COOKIES	Pg 25
16	EGGLESS COOKIES	Pg 26
17	CRIPSY BISCUIT	Pg 28
18	GULAM JAMUN	Pg 29
19	MILK POWEDER GULAM JAMUN	Pg 31
20	GULGULA	Pg 33
21	KALA JAMUN	Pg 35

ACKNOWLEDGMENTS

This book would have not been possible without support of my husband. From bottom of my heart I would like to thank my Husband Ajay Singh. My deepest gratitude to my mother who always supported me in everything, who taught me to become better person. I would like to thank my in-laws to encourage me and appreciate my cooking. I would like to thank my friends. I would like to thank everyone who helped me in every ways.
My recipes are simple and every ingredients are easily available in Indian kitchen. I believe in making food simple in terms of taste and in terms of flavours. Last but not least I would like to thank everyone who purchase my book and follow my recipes.

1 BESAN LADDU

Besan ke laddu is very yummy and popular. These sweets are made from roasted besan (gram flour), sugar and garnished with cashews and nuts. The crunchy texture and taste of these "Besan ke laddu" is very addictive and you might end of eating more than one every time.

INGREDIENTS:

- 2cups coarse gram flour (besan).
- 1-2 cup clarified butter(ghee).
- 11/2 cup of super fine granulated sugar.
- Water.
- ⅓ cup of sliced almonds, nuts or cashews

METHOD:

To start with, preheat the pan on medium heat. Add ½ cup of ghee and quantity later on.
Stir it well.
Ghee helps in adding flavour of the laddu and they last long for at least 1-2 months.
Now add 2 cups of gram flour you can use regular gram flour too, if you don't have coarse gram flour.
Make sure the flame is on medium heat and let the gram flour roast on low heat, stirring continuously to make sure the mixture didn't stick to the bottom of the wok pan.
Stir till gram flour started releasing the ghee.
Wait till it turns golden brown.
Once the ghee released.
Add 1 tablespoon ghee and keep stirring it.
Add ½ tablespoon of cardamom powder and keep stirring it.
Add few dry fruits mix it well.
Once the colour of the gram flour changes to light golden and a sweet aroma is released sprinkle some water.
Keep stirring and allow the water to evaporate.

Water sprinkle might cause small crumbs of gram flour to form

which gives a wonderful texture to the laddu.
Transfer the mixture to the tray or plate allow mixture to cool down a little, spread it on the tray to remove the heat from the mixture so that we can hold the besan in hands to make laddu.

Add 1 ½ cup fine granulated sugar(bhura). Make sure you use fine sugar.

Mix it well using your both hands.
Now grease both of your hands with little ghee and form small balls of the mixture.
Garnish with a pistachio on the center top you can garnish with kishmish too(raisin)

Store in airtight container.

ENJOY!

TIPS:

Always choose coarse grind gram flour for better taste.
If you don't have coarse grind gram flour, you can add 2 tablespoons of coarse semolina/ Rava in 1 cup of gram flour.
Roast gram flour on low flame this process will take some time have patience and roast to get perfect taste.

2 NACHNI AND OATS LADDU

Red millet or finger millet are known as ragi or nachni in most Indian languages. The best part of this laddu is it is full of carbohydrates along with protein and fiber. Nachni is healthy grain and should be included in the food that we make, being very rich in calcium it is excellent for kids and women. These laddus stay good for week at room temperature in a cool climate, In hot or humid climate refrigerate them.

INGREDIENTS:

- 1 cup nachni flour.
- ½ cup roasted oats flour.
- ½ cup jaggery.
- ½ cup ghee.
- 1 teaspoon cardamom powder.
- Cashews for decoration.

METHOD:
In a pan or wok add ghee when ghee melts add nachni flour and roast continuously on low sim.
Roast till ghee leaves and once the raw taste of nachni flour goes away, then add oats flour stir continuously for about 5 mins. Switched off the gas.
Keep on stirring for a min on, off the gas then add jaggery crumbs mix it well make sure there is no crumbs left of jaggery , it should be mix with flours well.
Add cardamom powder mix it well.
Transfer the mixture on a plate or big bowl.
Once the mixture turns warm and easy to handle, take small portion of it and make lemon size laddu and on the center top garnish with cashews or any nuts you like.

Store in jar.
Serve.

Enjoy and stay fit ☺

TIPS:

To get oats flour, first dry roast the oats on low flame, till raw taste goes away, then grind into grinder into fine powder.
Make sure that jaggery should be added after gas switched off, if you add before laddu will become hard.

3 SOOJI OR RAVA LADDU

Sooji k laddu/ Rava laddu.
Rava laddu is a simple and easy recipe but still exotic. Rava laddu is made with roasted Rava, ghee, sugar and nuts. It is very simple and tasty.

INGREDIENTS:

- 1 cup roasted sooji/semolina.
- 1 cup fine granulated sugar.
- 3-4 tablespoons clarified butter(ghee).
- Dry fruits of your choice.

METHOD:
Take a pan or wok add 2 tbsp ghee.
After ghee heat up add all dry nuts and saute them till they get nice golden colour, make sure flame should be on low sim.

Now add roasted sooji stir constantly on low flame for about 6-8 mins.
Add fine sugar and cardamom powder give it good mix and immediately off the flame.

Transfer on the plate, now let the mixture became warm then add 4-5 tbsp of milk mix the mixture gently.

Start making laddu

Store in fridge for 15-20 days.

TIPS:
Take fine Rava to make ladoo instead of regular one.
To get roasted rava,dry roast the rava in a pan on low flame till you get crunchy taste,do not over roast,otherwise the colour will change.

4 WHEAT OR CHURMA LADDU

Wheat flour laddu is also known as churma laddu. Basically it is made for Ganesh bhog during Ganesh chaturthi and during *Janmashtami*. Churma is made from whole coarse wheat flour, jaggery and ghee.

INGREDIENTS:

- 2 cups coarse whole wheat flour.
- 1 cup jaggery.
- ½ cup oil.
- ½ cup lukewarm ghee.
- 1 teaspoon cardamom powder.
- Lukewarm water for kneading.

METHOD:
In a large bowl take wheat flour, oil and give it good mix with the help of hand, it should form like breadcrumbs.
Now add lukewarm water gradually and start kneading into dough. Dough consistency should be tight.
Take 3 portion from dough, take 1 portion roll with help of roller pin into 6 to 7 cm diameter.

Place on medium hot tawa and roast well from both the side, it will take time to get cooked from inside. Make sure flame should be on low medium.
Repeat with other two doughs.

Now take all 3 roasted roti on a plate and broke into small pieces and grind into coarse powder.

Transfer the powder in bowl add cardamom and jaggery, mix well and make sure there is no lumps left, mix with hand.

Add lukewarm ghee mix it well and make laddus.

Store in airtight container.

ENJOY!

TIPS:
You can add dry fruits before adding ghee.
If one doesn't have coarse wheat flour, then go with regular wheat flour.

5 COCONUT BURFI

Coconut burfi is a classic and traditional recipe of an Indian sweet that is prepared during festivals and special occasion.

INGREDIENTS:

- 1 cup fresh mawa or khoya.
- 2 cups Dessicated coconut or coconut powder.
- 1 cup Sugar.
- 1 teaspoon clarified butter.
- ½ tablespoon of milk powder (optional)
- 1 cup water.

METHOD:

First make sugar syrup add sugar and water in a pan stir it, cook for a while keep on stirring, take a drop of sugar syrup between your fingers and check if a thread is forming then the sugar syrup is ready, flame should be on medium low flame throughout the procedure.

Now add mawa mix in the syrup make sure there is no lumps left, add cardamom powder,1 tablespoon ghee and mix it well, don't dry the mixture.
Keep on stirring for 5 minutes.
Transfer into grease tray or plate, flatten it with the help of spatula. Give slight cut to burfi and keep the tray in fridge for 1 hour, after 1 hour garnish it with almonds or pistachio.
Serve.

ENJOY!

TIPS:
One can add 2-3 tablespoons of milk powder, at the time of mixing coconut powder it is totally optional.
If you keep stirring even after the consistency reaches, then the sugar will get caramelized and colour will start to change.
You can use fresh grated coconut, here I have taken desiccated coconut.

6 KALAKAND BURFI

Kalakand burfi recipe is a traditional Indian sweet also known as milk cakes. Kalakand burfi is mostly made on Janmashtami, Diwali and some more festival occasions in India. This sweet is soft, tempering, healthy and tasty.

INGREDIENTS:

- ¾ cup thinly grated paneer (cottage cheese).
- 8 tablespoons milk powder.
- 1 teaspoon cornflour.
- ¼ cup sugar.
- ½ cup fresh cream for the garnish.
- ½ tsp cardamom powder (elaichi).
- 2 tablespoons almond (badam).

METHOD:

Combine all the ingredients in a microwave safe shallow dish and microwave on high for 5 minutes.
Spread the mixture in the same dish using the back of a spoon into an even layer.

Sprinkle the cardamom powder and chopped almonds evenly over it and keep aside to cool completely.
Cut into 18 equal pieces and refrigerate for at least an hour.

Serve chilled.

ENJOY!

TIPS:
Instead of microwave you can make in pan or wok.
If you are making in pan keep on stirring for 10 minutes do not over stir once done transfer into tray and follow the same steps.

   here. Insert chapter six text here. Insert chapter six text here. Insert chapter six text here. Insert chapter six text here. Insert chapter six text

7 AUTHENTIC MAWA GUJHIYA/KHOYA KARANJI

It is traditional sweet dumpling. It is made on Holi as well as on Deepawali specially in North India. Different region has different name and stuffing. The outer layer is crispy yet flaky in texture. While the stuffing is very rich and sweet made from mawa, sooji, fine sugar and nuts.

INGREDIENTS:

For outer cover:
- 2 cups of maida (all purpose flour).
- 2 tbsp ghee (clarified butter).
- 2 pinch salt.
- 1 cup water.

For Stuffing:
- 250 grams mawa (khoya).
- 100 grams roasted sooji (semolina).
- 1 teaspoon green cardamom seeds powder.
- 2 pinch freshly grated nutmeg.
- 125 grams fine powder sugar.
- 75 grams chironji. (piyal seeds)
- Enough oil for frying.

METHOD:

Heat the mava in a pan on medium heat.
Keep stirring continuously, it will start to melt. Cook till it becomes light brown, turn off the gas. It took 5-6 mins.
Remove it to a big bowl let it cools down completely, now add sugar, cardamom powder, nutmeg, chironji. Mix it well using your fingertips make sure there is no lumps left.
Keep the stuffing aside.

Making outer cover for Gujhiya:

Mix all purpose flour and salt drizzle ghee and rub it into flour using

your fingertips It will be breadcrumbs like texture.
Start adding little water at a time.
Knead the dough into stiff and smooth dough. Cover it and let it rest for 15 minutes.

After 15 minutes knead the dough once again and divide it into lemon size equal portion.
Roll into a thin into a 4-inch diameter circle.
Put about a tablespoon stuffing in the centre.
Apply little water around the edges using your finger.
Fold it into half circle (like semicircle). Seal the edges by pressing it.
If it is not seals properly then it will open up while frying and it will be big mess.
Make all gujiyas and cover them with towel to prevent it from drying out.
Heat the oil in a wok on medium heat.
Once it is hot enough then fry 2-3 at a time don't overcrowded flip in between for even browsing.

Once it is golden brown and crispy from all sides remove it on paper towel.
When cools down completely store in airtight container.

ENJOY!

TIPS:

Knead the dough properly to get crispy and flaky texture, don't add too much ghee or oil while kneading otherwise it will break in the oil, follow the quantity what I mentioned.
Fill small amount of stuffing.

8 GUJIYA OR KARANJI STUFFING

This stuffing is different from authentic mawa stuffing. In India Maharashtra most of people make this type of stuffing using desiccated coconut. It tastes very delicious and rich.

INGREDIENTS:

- 1 bowl desiccated coconut.
- ½ bowl semolina/rava
- ¼ cup poppy seed/khas khas.
- ¼ cup sesame seeds/Til.
- 2 bowl fine powdered sugar.
- 1-½ teaspoon cardamom powder.
- 2 teaspoons clarified butter/ghee.
- Raisin and chironji as per required. (Raisins and piyal seeds)
- Pinch of salt.

METHOD:

First roast desiccated coconut in heated pan on slow flame, continuously stir it.
Do not over roast otherwise its colour will get spoil.
Remove in mixing bowl.
Now in same pan add 2 teaspoon of ghee and roast rava on slow flame, roast for a minute transfer into same mixing bowl.
Dry roast khas khas for minute, transfer in mixing bowl.
Roast raisins and piyal for a minute, transfer in mixing bowl.
Roast sesame for a minute, transfer in mixing bowl.
Switch off the gas.
In mixture add powder sugar, cardamom powder, pinch of salt and with the help of hand combine all mixtures together.
Make sure there is no lumps.

Follow the same procedure of gujiya outer cover fill the stuffings and fry follow the instruction of mawa gujiya.

Store in airtight container.

ENJOY!

TIPS:
Do not over roast any given ingredients.
Fill 1 teaspoon of stuffing's, otherwise it will get open while frying, sealed it properly.
While adding fine sugar sieve it, it will remove all lumps.

9 SHANKARPALI

Shankarpali is a sweet biscuits made during Diwali festivals. Its taste very yummy. It is made from all purpose flour, semolina and sugar.

INGREDIENTS:
- 1.5 cups of maida (all purpose flour).
- ½ cup of sooji (semolina).
- ½ cup powdered sugar.
- 1 pinch salt.
- 3-3.5 tablespoon milk or as required.
- Oil for frying.

METHOD:
Mix all dry ingredients well then add 2 tablespoons of melted ghee, again mix the flour you will get breadcrumbs like texture.
Knead nicely with hand, then add each tablespoon of warm milk gradually and knead to a tight firm dough.
If the dough looks dry, then add ½ or 1 teaspoon of warm milk and knead again.
Keep for rest, cover the dough with paper towel to prevent it from drying.
Divide the dough into two equal parts roll one part into 6 to 7 inches diameter.
Cut in diamond shape.
Fry the 8 to 10 slice at time time, drain on paper towel.
Store in airtight container.

ENJOY!

TIPS:
You can bake also,for baking keep shankarpali slices in baking tray bake in Preheat oven to 180 Deg C for 10 to 12 mins till golden on the edges.They will turn crispy as they cool.
While baking first portion of batch keep other portion in fridge do not forget to cover the dough.

10 BUTTER CHAKLI

Butter chakli just melts in mouth. It is crunchy and savoury Indian snacks prepared during festival seasons. It is very good and yummy snacks at tea time also.

INGREDIENTS:

- 1 cup rice flour.
- 1 cup water.
- ½ teaspoon cumin seeds or jeera.
- 50 grams butter.
- 1 teaspoon white sesame seeds or til.
- 4-5 crushed green chillies.

METHOD:

Take a deep bowl add water once the water starts boiling add butter stir it well add cumin, salt, green chillies stir constantly.
Now switch off the gas.
After switching off the gas add sesame and flour mix to the hot water gently mix with spoon, cover the lid and rest it for half an hour.
After half an hour, transfer the mixture on plate and start kneading the dough.
Take a chakli mould, grease the mould take half portion of dough, make chakli on foil.

Gently drop 2-3 chaklis on medium hot oil on low flame.
Fry the chakli light golden colour.
Take out on paper towel.

Cool at room temperature.

Store in airtight container.

ENJOY!

TIPS:
Water and rice measurements should be equal to get perfect butter chakli.
Do not over fry, fry till they get crispy.
Hear I have used normal amul butter.

11 MASALA CHAKLI

There are many variations of chaklis made in India. Rice flour chakli is crisp, crunchy, mouth-watering instant snacks. It is usually made during Deepawali festival. Chakli also known as Murukku in south India. Spiral shaped snacks that is deep fried. Here I have made chaklis from rice flour.

INGREDIENTS:

- 1 cup rice flour (chawal ka ata).
- ½ teaspoon coriander powder. (dhaniya powder).
- ½ teaspoon red chilli powder (lal mirch powder).
- ¼ teaspoon carom seeds(ajwain).
- ½ teaspoon sesame seeds(til)
- ¼ teaspoon turmeric powder (haldi powder).
- Oil for frying.

METHOD:
In a bowl add all dry ingredients give it good mix.

When everything is well combined add 1 teaspoon of oil again mix it well.
Add 1 cup of hot water give it good mix, cover it for 5 minutes, after 5 minutes transfer into plate and knead into soft dough.
Cover the dough and rest it for ½ an hour.

After half an hour, knead once again.
Take a chakli mould grease some oil and start making round chakli on foil or on greased plate, make sure when you drop one chakli, sealed the edges so while frying it will not break, and get perfect chakli.

Fry the chakli on medium hot oil, cook evenly till you get golden colour, make sure oil is hot enough.
Drain on paper towel.

Store in airtight container.

ENJOY!

TIPS:
Drop the chakli with the help of spatula slowly in hot oil.
If you feel dough is stiff and not able to combine,add little hot water and knead it.

12 WHEAT CHAKLI

Wheat flour chakli is a traditional way of making instant chaklis where the flour is cooked in pressure cooker before making chaklis. It is very delicious and healthy.
INGREDIENTS:

- 1 cup whole wheat flour.
- 2 ½ teaspoons red chilli powder.
- 1 teaspoon coriander seed powder.
- 1 teaspoon cumin powder.
- ½ teaspoon turmeric powder.
- 1 teaspoon asafoetida.
- 2 teaspoons white sesame seeds.
- Salt to taste.
- Oil for frying.

METHOD:

Take muslin cloth or any clean cotton cloth.
Place the flour in a clean white muslin or any clean cotton cloth.
Tie it up like a pouch.

Put 1 glass of water in pressure cooker and put one plate on top of the ring.
Now place flour pouch and steam it for 20 mins remove the whistle and cover the lid.
After 20 minutes open the lid of the cooker untie the wheat pouch.

Transfer the wheat into the plate break the hard flour with the help of hand.
Make sure there is no lumps left.
Now add all the dry ingredients mention above.

Give it good mix.
Add 1 teaspoon of hot oil and mix it well.
Make sure add only 1 teaspoon of oil, if you add more oil then while frying chakli will break.
Start kneading dough by using little water.
Dough should be stiff yet smooth and non-sticky dough.
Use star hole plate mould grease it,add half portion of the dough inside mould and seal it properly.
Start making chakli on foil/plastic paper.
Make 3-4 chakli in batches.
Fry chakli on hot oil then only chakli will be crispy.

Deep fry both side until crisp and golden brown.
Drain over a paper towel.
When cools down completely store in an air tight container.

ENJOY

TIPS:
Fry the chakli on hot oil.
At a time fry 2 to 3 chakli,once done one side then only flip other side and cook.

13 GATHIYA

An easy to make savoury snacks recipes that you can make for your friends and family on get together and during festivals. Gathiya is delicious and tasty. You can also enjoy this as an evening snacks too!

INGREDIENTS:

- ½ cup oil
- ½ cup water.
- 1 teaspoon asafoetida.
- 1 tablespoon salt.
- 1 tablespoon carom seeds/ajwain.
- 3 cups gram flour/besan.
- Oil for frying.

METHOD:

Take oil and water in a bowl, add asafoetida, salt and ajwain stir this mixture well with hand until oil and water combined well and give thick consistency.
Now add besan into the water oil mixture, mix all together well and form into dough.
Take oil on heating pan, oil should be hot enough.
Grease the jhara apply some oil place handful of besan dough and with the help of palm rub on all side, you will see thin long gathiya will drop in hot oil.
Keep aside the jhara and fry the gathiya in light golden colour.
Remove on paper towel.
Follow same with remaining dough.

Cools down completely.
Store in airtight container.

ENJOY!

TIPS:
Quantity of oil and water should be same.
If you do not have jhara then you can use gathiya maker mould, use small hole plate in the mould.

14 POHA CHIVDA

An easy to make savoury snacks recipes that you can make for your friends and family on get together and during festivals. Gathiya is delicious and tasty. You can also enjoy this as an evening snacks too!

INGREDIENTS:

- ½ cup oil
- ½ cup water.
- 1 teaspoon asafoetida.
- 1 tablespoon salt.
- 1 tablespoon carom seeds/ajwain.
- 3 cups gram flour/besan.
- Oil for frying.

METHOD:

Take oil and water in a bowl, add asafoetida, salt and ajwain stir this mixture well with hand until oil and water combined well and give thick consistency.

Now add besan into the water oil mixture, mix all together well and form into dough.
Take oil on heating pan, oil should be hot enough.
Grease the jhara apply some oil place handful of besan dough and with the help of palm rub on all side, you will see thin long gathiya will drop in hot oil.
Keep aside the jhara and fry the gathiya in light golden colour.
Remove on paper towel.
Follow same with remaining dough.

Cools down completely.
Store in airtight container.

ENJOY!

TIPS:
Before making chivda, sift poha well and sundry for at least 3 to 4 hours, by doing this it will take less time to cook, and gives fast crunchy texture.
One can add dry nuts also.

15 ALOMOND DROP COOKIES

Almond drop cookies are just like biscuits, it is very light and tasty with the flavour of almonds.

INGREDIENTS:

- 2 cups amul plain butter, softened.
- 3-½ cups all-purpose flour(maida).
- 2 tsp almond extract.
- 2 cups sugar.
- 1 tsp baking soda.
- ½ tsp salt.
- 1 cup sliced almonds.

METHOD:

In a large bowl, mix butter and sugar until light and fluffy. Beat in extract.
Sift flour, baking powder, baking soda and salt; gradually add to creamed mixture. Stir in almonds, mix flour in creamed mixture very gently don't beat it.
Drop by rounded teaspoonful's 2 inches apart onto ungreased baking sheets.
Bake at high for 10-13 minutes or until lightly browned.

Cool for 2 minutes before removing to wire racks.

Store in airtight container.

ENJOY!

16 EGGLESS COOKIES

Microwave Eggless Cookies is crunchy and yummy biscuits. It is good snacks at tea time. Nothing much to say about these cookies just give them try and enjoy!

INGREDIENTS:

- 1-¼ cup All-purpose flour.
- ¼ cup Gram flour (besan).
- 1-½ tablespoons Thin Semolina (sooji).
- 1 cup clarified butter (ghee).
- 1 teaspoon cardamom powder.
- 1 cup fine sugar powder.
- 10-15 Almonds slit from middle for garnishing.
- 1-¼ teaspoon of baking powder.

METHOD:

Sieve all dry ingredients into bowl, sieving helps to break all the lumps and to get fine flour.
Now in another bowl gently mix ghee and sugar, then with the help of beater or hand grinder beat into fluffy texture.
Now add flour into the ghee mixture slowly mix it add cardamom powder and mix gently.
Knead into very soft dough with the help of hand.
Before making the dough preheat the oven on 180 degrees for 10 mins.

Divide the dough into two equal parts and keep one part in the fridge, so it will be easy to handled.
And from one part cut lemon size equal ball and on the centre press slice almond, slightly press, do all remaining same way.
Now keep in grease baking tray and bake for about 20 minutes.
After 20 minutes off the oven and let it rest on rack for 5 minutes.
Bursting with flavour, these cookies will just melt in your mouth.

I have baked two batches one is a lighter baked for 12 to 15 minutes and another one is a darker batch baked for 15 to 20 minutes.

ENJOY!

TIPS:
While kneading dough,if you feel dough is dry then add 1 tablespoon of cold milk.
When first part is finished baking,remove the second portion from the fridge and bake the same way.
When first part is baked remove another portion from the fridge and baked it.

17 CRISPY BISCUIT

Crispy biscuits is very tasty and good snacks with a cup of hot tea. It is also made during friends and relatives get together.

INGREDIENTS:

- 100 grams all-purpose flour.
- 2 tablespoons chopped dry fenugreek (kasuri methi).
- ½ tablespoon sugar.
- ½ tablespoon cumin seeds(jeera).
- ½ teaspoon crushed black pepper. (kali miri).
- ¼ teaspoon turmeric powder(haldi).
- 5 tablespoons oil.
- Salt as required.
- 5 tablespoons curd.

METHOD:

In a bowl add all purpose flour(maida), cumin seed, turmeric, sugar, black pepper, fenugreek dry. Give it good mix then add 5 tablespoons curd,5 tablespoons oil mix it with the help of hand and make dough without adding water.
Rest the dough for 10-15 minutes.
Divide the dough in 3 parts, roll the dough portion like chapati.
With the help of cutter cut into diamond shape.
Take ungreased microwave tray keep the slices little apart.
Now on high rack preheat the oven on 180 degrees.
Bake for 12 mins.
After 12 min take out from tray and let it rest for 5 to 10 mins.

Store in the container.

ENJOY!

TIPS:
Instead of black pepper you can add ¼ teaspoon red chilli powder.

18 GULAB JAMUN

A classic Indian sweet or dessert that is very famous and is enjoyed in most festival and celebration meals.

INGREDIENTS:

- For gulab jamun dough.
- 250 grams fresh khoya.
- 50 grams ararot ka aata(Arrowroot flour)
- Cold milk to knead the dough.
- For sugar syrup:
- 500 grams sugar.
- 500 grams water.
- Few strand of kesar(optional).
- 2-3 green cardamom crushed.

METHOD:

First take pan add sugar and water stir it on medium flame.
Add cardamom in syrup, kesar mix it.
Once sugar melts well switched off the gas.
Make sure we don't want thread form consistency, just sugar should melts properly.

For dough:
Grate mawa or khoya add ararot four mix gently then by adding milk gradually knead a soft dough, don't worry if dough gets sticky.
Do not over knead the mixture just lightly mix it, if you over mix it, gluten forms and jamun will turn dense and will not absorb sugar syrup properly.
Grease your palm with ghee or oil divide minutes into marble size small balls.
Make all crack free balls cover with paper towel.
Fry the balls on normal hot oil on low sim, when you will drop the balls make sure don't immediately flip it let it rest in oil for minute or two.
With the help of spoon on spatula stir the oil not balls, let balls turn

itself, then gently start mo ving the balls in oil and fry from all side.
Remove the jamun and drop in warm sugar syrup.
Let it rest for 2 to 3 hours in sugar syrup.

Check in between all the jamuns have suck the syrup.
For sugar syrup follow recipes of kala or gulab jamun.
While serving take 2 to 3 gulab jamuns on plate.

Store in fridge.

19 MILK POWDER GULAB JAMUN

Gulab jamuns need no introduction it is very popular sweet dish in Indian and it is made during special occasion and it is loved by everyone. Sweet, tasty and mouth-watering dish. Here I am sharing you gulab jamuns made from milk powder and it is very good for beginners to start with. If mawa or khoya is not easily available in most places and is very tedious to make at home, then try this gulab jamuns recipe and this will also give you the equal taste like mawa jamuns.

INGREDIENTS:

- ½ cup milk powder.
- 1 tablespoon all-purpose flour or maida.
- ⅛ teaspoon baking soda.
- 1 tablespoon clarified butter or ghee.
- 2 tablespoons milk.
- For sugar syrup:
- Sugar.
- Water
- Green cardamom crushed or 2 pinch cardamom powder.

METHOD:

For dough:
Take milk powder, maida, baking soda in a bowl mix well make sure there is no lumps better seive it.
Now add ghee, use your hand to mix it so that ghee mixes evenly with milk powder and gently mix it.
If required add few more teaspoon of milk and mix lightly.
Dough should be soft it may be sticky but do not worry about it.
Do not over mix it, if you over mix it, gluten forms and jamun will turn dense and will not absorb sugar syrup.
Grease your palm divide mixture into marble size small portion around 9-10.
Make crack free balls.
Fry on low flame on medium hot oil, once done drop in sugar syrup

for 2 to 3 hours.
Take the jamuns while serving.

Store in fridge.

ENJOY!

TIPS:
Make sure fry the jamuns on low flame on medium hot oil, have patience and fry it will take time to cook from inside
NOTE: Follow the sugar recipes and instructions from my other gulab or kala jamuns.

20 GULGULA

Gulgulas are like lightly sweetened mini donuts. Gulgula is a dessert made during special occasion like Diwali and wedding ceremony. It is also serve to God as bhog. This is an easy recipe to make your craving for something sweet.

INGREDIENTS:

- 1 cup whole wheat flour.
- ⅓ cup sugar or as required sweet.
- Cold milk.
- 1 tablespoon fennel seeds.
- ½ teaspoon cardamom powder.
- OIl for frying.

METHOD:

Take a bowl add flour, sugar, cardamom powder, fennel seeds or saunf give it good mix.

Gradually add little Little milk and stir it well till you gets thick pouring consistency.

Cover the batter and keep for rest at least 2 to 3 hours.
In a pan add oil, once the oil heated up add small balls deep fry till you gets golden brown color.
Fry the gulgulas golden brown all sides, turning them occasionally. It will take 2 to 3 minutes.

Remove the gulgulas over paper towel.
Flame should be on low medium flame.
Serve hot or warm
Store in fridge for 2 to 3 days.

ENJOY!

TIPS:
you can add dry fruits also in the batter.
If oil is not hot enough gulgulas will stick it the bottom of the frying pan.
The frying pan should have about 1 inch of oil (To check if oil is ready,put one drop of batter in oil.The batter should come up but not change colour right away).
You can keep the batter for half an hour also if you want make urgent.
For better gulgulas keep for rest at least 2 to 3 hours

21 KALA JAMUN

Kala jamun is same as gulab jamun only the difference is it is dark colour to get dark brown colour. It is very tasty and rich authentic sweet dish.

INGREDIENTS:

- 500 grams fresh mawa.
- 50 grams maida (all purpose flour)
- 1 teaspoon cardamom powder.
- 500 grams sugar.
- 500 lit water.
- Few strand of kesar(optional).

METHOD:

Grate mawa in big bowl, add cardamom powder and maida mix well and form into soft dough (without adding milk).
Make lemon size fine balls in a plate and cover with paper towel.
Now heat oil in kadhai. Flame should be low and oil should be low medium heat.
Take 1 ball dust into maida flour roll again and drop into low medium heat.

At a time drop 2 to 3 jamuna only, let it cook slowly don't touch the balls with spoon otherwise it will break, just stir the oil, jamuns will be float of it owns.
Cook till you will get dark brown color.
Once the balls float of its own then start stirring with spoon slowly continuously till you get dark brown color.
Take out from kadai and drop into warm syrup, let it rest for hour.

For syrup:
Boil sugar, water and cardamom powder or 2-3 crushed. Once melt completely switched off the flame. add few strand of kesar.

Serve cold.

ENJOY!

TIPS:
Just stir and melt the sugar syrup,don't form in thread consistency, otherwise jamun will become hard.

About The Author

Rekkha Ajay Singh is basically from Mumbai, now moved to Pune. Cooking has always been her passion. She tries to focus on easy approachable recipes with ingredients you can find in regular grocery stores. Her cooking Master is her Mom, and she follows what she has learn from her mother i.e " Good and tasty food doesn't needs more ingredients as it diminishes the main ingredient of food".

So She wants to share this experience with one and all. With God's grace and support from her husband a website and a Youtube channel is created to upload cooking videos.

She says, I am not a chef, I want to follow my passion and want to share with you all my everyday recipes straight from my kitchen and am not an expert I am a learner and will be a learner throughout my life!.

And She promise to share delicious, quick and easy recipes :)

Printed in Great Britain
by Amazon